JAPAN

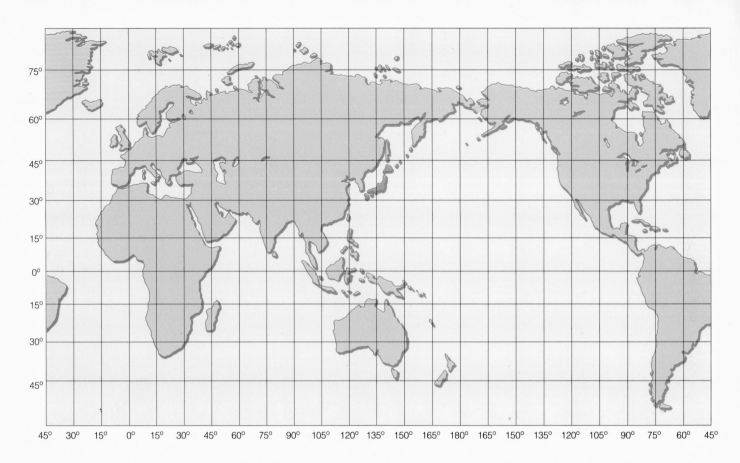

135°

RUSSIA

HOKKAIDO

Kushiro

Otaru • Sapporo

IINA

RTH
REA

SEA

OF

JAPAN

Aomori

40°

Akita • Morioka

H O N S H U

Sendai

Niigata

Hitachi

TOKYO

Chiba

Fukui

Kawasaki
Yokohama

Lake Biwa

Nagoya

Matsue

Kyoto

UTH
REA

Kobe

Okayama

Osaka

S E A

Hiroshima

INLAND

Tokushima

TSU
ISLANDS

Kochi

Kitakyushu

SHIKOKU

JAPAN

N

Fukuoka

W   E

Kumamoto

S

Nagasaki

Kagoshima

KYUSHU

0   100 mi

RYUKYU

160 km

ISLANDS

P A C I F I C   O C E A N

KOREA STRAIT

John Baines

RAINTREE STECK-VAUGHN
P U B L I S H E R S

Austin, Texas

Published by Raintree Steck-Vaughn Publishers, an imprint of
Steck-Vaughn Company

Design	Roger Kohn
Editor	Penny Clarke, Helene Resky
DTP editor	Helen Swansbourne
Picture research	Valerie Mulcahy
Illustration	János Márffy
	Coral Mula
Calligraphy	Suzuko Nakajima
Translation	Yuuichiro Nakajima
Special thanks	John Buchanan

We are grateful to the following for permission
to reproduce photographs:
Front Cover: Peter Rauter/TRIP, *below,* Robert Harding Picture
Library, *above;* Camera Press, pages 19 (Jung Kwan Chi), 35
below (Peter Abbey/LNS); J. Allan Cash, pages 18 *above,* 20,
21, 29, 30; Colorific!, pages 17 (Mike Yamashita), 33 (Eiji
Miyazawa/Black Star); Eye Ubiquitous/TRIP, pages 27 *inset*
and 28 (Frank Leather), 35 *above* (Paul Thompson);
Greenpeace, page 39 (Morgan); Robert Harding Picture
Library, pages 25, 26, 27 *below;* The Image Bank, pages 36
below (Jules Zalon), 38 (G. Colliva); Japan National Tourist
Organization, page 13; Magnum, pages 18 *below* (Ian Berry),
22 (Bruno Barbey), 36 *above* (Paul Fusco); Nissan Motor
Manufacturing (U.K.) Ltd., pages 31, 32; Orion Press, pages 8,
9, 12, 37; Peter Rauter/TRIP, page 42; Rex Features/Sipa-
Press, page 24 (Toyosaki); Tony Stone Worldwide, pages 15
(Thierry Cazabon), 16 (Matthew Harris), 23 *below,* 27 *above,*
40; Taisei Corporation, page 41; Telegraph Colour Library,
pages 11 (VCL), 23 *above;* Toyota AG, page 43; Yamaha-
Kemble Music (U.K.) Ltd., page 34; Yamaha Motor Europe,
page 34 *below;* Zefa, page 14 (Goebel).

The statistics given in this book are the most up to date
available at the time of going to press

Printed and bound in Hong Kong by
Paramount Printing Group Ltd

1 2 3 4 5 6 7 8 9 0 HK 99 98 97 96 95 94

Library of Congress Cataloging-in-Publication Data

Baines, John D.
Japan / written by John Baines.
p. cm. — (Country fact files)
Includes index.
Summary: Examines the landscape, climate, natural
resources, population, daily life, and government of Japan.
ISBN 0-8114-1847-2
1. Japan—Juvenile literature. I. Title. II. Series
DS806.B24 1994
952—dc20
93-23948
CIP

Words that are explained in the glossary are printed in
SMALL CAPITALS the first time they are mentioned in the text.

**C
O
N
T
E
N
T
S**

INTRODUCTION

The Japanese word for Japan, *Nippon*, means "source of the sun," from which comes a popular Western nickname for Japan: land of the rising sun. Today we are more likely to think of Japan as the home of electronic goods, motorcycles, cameras, and countless makes of cars. All these things play a very important part in our lives and in the economies of all Western countries. But these are really very recent developments.

Japan is an old country with ancient traditions. These traditions are very different from those of other countries because Japan remained isolated from outside influences until after 1854. The traditions remain, although the Japanese way of life has changed dramatically.

Japan is now a highly successful industrial nation and shares many similarities with other major industrial countries including large, crowded cities with congested streets, high-rise buildings,

▼ *The ritual of the tea ceremony or* cha-no-yu *is 600 years old. It is held in a simple room. By concentrating on the tea-making the participants aim to achieve a feeling of peacefulness.*

shops, offices, and factories. The people are well-off and live in comfortable homes. Their health care and education systems are good. But there are environmental problems like those in other developed countries: loss of countryside, traffic congestion, air pollution, and water pollution.

This book is an introduction to Japan. You will find information about the country and its people, the climate and the natural resources, and how the Japanese earn their livings and spend their leisure time. The Japanese economic success story is something we cannot afford to ignore.

JAPAN AT A GLANCE

- Area: 145,870 square miles (377,803 sq km)
- Population: about 124 million
- Density: about 854 people per square mile (320 people per sq km)
- Capital: Tokyo, population 8.1 million
- Other main cities: Yokohama 3.2 million; Osaka 2.6 million; Nagoya 2.1 million; Sapporo 1.6 million; Kyoto 1.4 million
- Highest mountain: Mount Fuji, 12,388 feet (3,776 m)
- Language: Japanese
- Main religions: Shintoism, Buddhism, Christianity
- Currency: YEN, written as ¥
- Economy: Highly industrialized
- Major natural resources: Fish, timber, fast-flowing rivers
- Major products: Automobiles, electrical and electronic goods, textiles, steel, machines and robots, rice
- Environment: Severe pollution of air, water, and land near industrial areas, but controls are now much stricter

◀ The crowded streets of Tokyo are similar to any big modern city.

THE LANDSCAPE

Japan is a country made up of islands. There are four large ones: Hokkaido, Honshu, Shikoku, and Kyushu, and about 3,000 much smaller ones. The islands run north to south for over 1,553 miles (2,500 km). To the west about 311 miles (500 km) across the Sea of Japan is the mainland of Asia. To the east the nearest countries to Japan are the United States and Canada about 4,347 miles (7,000 km) away across the Pacific Ocean.

Mountains cover about 70 percent of Japan. Fast-flowing rivers have cut steep narrow valleys into their sides, and there are many beautiful lakes along the valleys. The east coast is rugged and has many inlets, in contrast to the west coast, which has long sweeping shores. There is little flat land. Only 15 percent of Japan is level enough for farming and building. Small plains occur around the coast. The Kanto Plain is one of the largest. It is where Tokyo, the capital of Japan, is located.

Volcanoes are found all over Japan. Although many are extinct, geologists believe 67 are still active. The most famous is Mount Fuji, which, at 12,388 feet (3,776 m), is Japan's highest mountain.

Every year in Japan there are hundreds of

▶ *Japan is a very mountainous and beautiful country with varied scenery. The mountains of the interior contrast with a coastline of cliffs, inlets, and sweeping bays.*

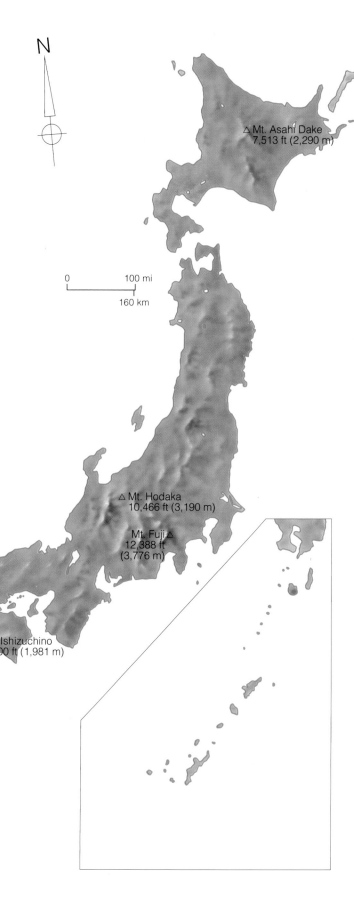

N

0   100 mi
160 km

△ Mt. Asahi Dake
7,513 ft (2,290 m)

△ Mt. Hodaka
10,466 ft (3,190 m)

Mt. Fuji △
12,388 ft
(3,776 m)

△ Mt. Ishizuchino
6,500 ft (1,981 m)

△ Mt. Kuju
5,861 ft (1,787 m)

◀ *Of all the Shinto religious sites, Mount Fuji is the most sacred because of its beauty and size.*

KEY FACTS

● Japan is roughly one and a half times the size of the state of Montana.
● No part of Japan is more than 75 miles (121 km) from the sea.
● Japan has about 20,000 hot springs.
● Japan has 67 active volcanoes; geologists watch 17 constantly in case they show signs of erupting.
● Mount Fuji last erupted in 1707.
● Japan has four earthquakes a day, but few are even felt.

earthquakes. Many are very small, but it is quite common for buildings to sway and ornaments to fall off shelves. However, this has not stopped the Japanese from building skyscrapers. They are designed to sway gently as the ground moves, so they do not collapse. Occasionally there are strong earthquakes, which cause terrible damage. Tokyo was destroyed by one in 1923. The city caught fire, and 143,000 people died. This earthquake also caused a tidal wave 33 feet (10 m) high which swept inland causing more death and destruction.

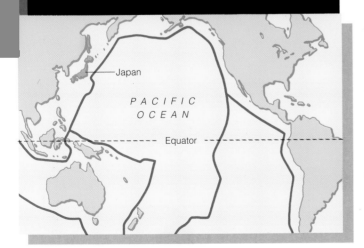

◀ *The Earth's crust consists of several plates. Around the Pacific, earthquakes and volcanic activity occur where plates meet. This area is known as the Pacific Ring, here marked in red.*

(11)

CLIMATE AND WEATHER

Japan lies between latitudes 24°N and 45°N. The difference is the same as between the Canadian city of Montreal and the Gulf of Mexico. In the north the summers are short, cool, and damp and the winters long and cold with snow lying on the ground for up to four months a year. In the south temperatures are about 27°F (15°C) higher throughout the year. In Sapporo on Hokkaido the temperature ranges between 20°F (-6°C) and 68°F (20°C); in Okinawa in the south the range is 50°F (10°C) to 90°F (32°C).

Seasonal winds, called monsoons, cause differences in the climate between the west and east coasts. Cold winter winds from the mainland of Asia bring rain and snow to the west coast. Niigata has 7.5 inches (194 mm) of rain and snow in January. The east coast is still cold and windy but is much drier and brighter. Tokyo only averages about 2 inches (48 mm) of rain and snow each winter.

In summer warm, moist winds blow across Japan from the Pacific Ocean. They are very humid and with the summer heat, the weather can be very uncomfortable.

Ocean currents also influence the climate. A branch of the warm Japan Current from the tropics passes along the shores of western Japan. It warms the cold air blowing from the mainland in winter. Warm air absorbs more moisture than cold air, and this increases winter rainfall on the west coast. The cold Oyashio Current from the Arctic runs along the east of Hokkaido, and where it meets the warm current, there are bad fogs.

The seasons are very important to the Japanese, especially spring and the flowering of the cherry trees. Newspapers report where and when the trees are at their best.

▼ *Typhoons regularly hit Japan, mainly between July and November. They start over the southwest Pacific as small areas of low pressure. By the time they reach Japan, the very strong winds spiral upward and cause much damage.*

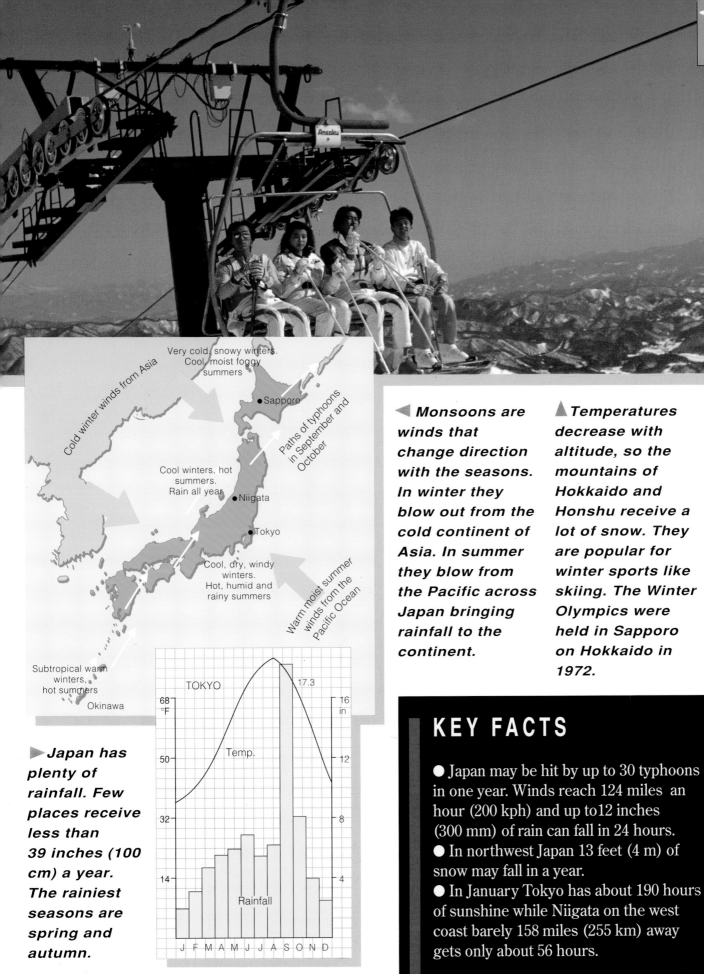

Very cold, snowy winters.
Cool, moist foggy
summers

Cold winter winds from Asia

Paths of typhoons
in September and
October

• Sapporo

Cool winters, hot
summers.
Rain all year

• Niigata

• Tokyo

Cool, dry, windy
winters.
Hot, humid and
rainy summers

Warm moist summer
winds from the
Pacific Ocean

Subtropical warm
winters,
hot summers

Okinawa

TOKYO

17.3

68
°F

16
in

Temp.

50

12

32

8

14

4

Rainfall

J F M A M J J A S O N D

◀ **Monsoons are winds that change direction with the seasons. In winter they blow out from the cold continent of Asia. In summer they blow from the Pacific across Japan bringing rainfall to the continent.**

▲ **Temperatures decrease with altitude, so the mountains of Hokkaido and Honshu receive a lot of snow. They are popular for winter sports like skiing. The Winter Olympics were held in Sapporo on Hokkaido in 1972.**

▶ **Japan has plenty of rainfall. Few places receive less than 39 inches (100 cm) a year. The rainiest seasons are spring and autumn.**

KEY FACTS

● Japan may be hit by up to 30 typhoons in one year. Winds reach 124 miles an hour (200 kph) and up to 12 inches (300 mm) of rain can fall in 24 hours.

● In northwest Japan 13 feet (4 m) of snow may fall in a year.

● In January Tokyo has about 190 hours of sunshine while Niigata on the west coast barely 158 miles (255 km) away gets only about 56 hours.

NATURAL RESOURCES

Japan is an economic superpower like the United States. The United States and Japan are the world's main industrial countries. Unlike the U.S., Japanese industry does not have the advantage of large local supplies of fossil fuels or raw materials. Fossil fuels, such as coal and oil, provide energy to produce metals from raw materials, like iron ore, and to drive machines that make products, like cars and TV sets.

Japan has very little coal. There are mines on the islands of Hokkaido and Kyushu, but the coal is of poor quality and expensive to mine. Small deposits of oil are found under the land and the ocean in northern Japan. However, most coal and oil are imported.

Japan's energy comes mainly from oil (57 percent) and coal (18 percent). Coal and oil are used to generate about half of the country's electricity. Water power (hydro-electricity) and nuclear power generate the rest. Japan is developing nuclear power plants to avoid relying on imported fossil fuels (coal and oil). In 1991 there were 39 working nuclear power plants, 11 more

The Chiba iron and steel plant. Plants like this use huge quantities of natural resources.

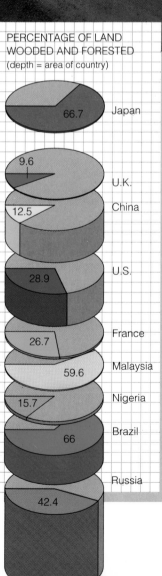

PERCENTAGE OF LAND WOODED AND FORESTED
(depth = area of country)

66.7	Japan
9.6	U.K.
12.5	China
28.9	U.S.
26.7	France
59.6	Malaysia
15.7	Nigeria
66	Brazil
42.4	Russia

KEY FACTS

● Sixty-seven percent of Japan is covered with forests. It is the tenth most forested country in the world.
● Japan mines 105,792 tons of iron ore a year but uses 137 million tons.
● Japan produces one percent of the oil and eleven percent of the natural gas it uses.
● Japan imports raw materials, like iron ore, and exports manufactured products, like cars and electrical goods.

▲*The Kurobe Dam in the Japanese Alps makes hydroelectricity using the energy of falling water. With steep-sided valleys, fast-flowing streams, and plentiful rainfall, Japan can produce a quarter of its electricity in this way.*

being built, and three others in the planning stages. These power plants need only a few pounds of uranium fuel to operate instead of thousands of tons of oil or coal.

Japan produces few of the raw materials it needs. It mines small quantities of iron ore, copper, zinc, lead, gold, and silver. Although it produces very few raw materials, Japan is the world's second-largest consumer of tin and the third-largest consumer of iron ore, oil, and rubber.

Japan is one of the most forested countries of the world, but it still has to import timber. Some of Japan's timber comes from the tropical rain forests in nearby countries, such as Malaysia and Indonesia. Environmentalists are worried that logging is destroying these forests, the wildlife, and the ways of life of people who live there. Timber is also imported from North America.

● POPULATION

Almost everyone in Japan has similar physical characteristics. This is because most people are descended from the immigrants who came from the mainland of Asia and settled in southwest Japan. In general the Japanese have straight black hair, medium-colored skin, dark brown or black eyes, and very little hair on their faces or bodies.

Because Japan is so mountainous, most people settled on the small plains around the coast. They gathered in villages and small towns, making their living from farming and fishing.

Over the last 100 years the population has grown from around 40 million to 124 million, but about 90 percent of the people still live on the coastal plains. The plains between Tokyo and Kyushu are among the most densely populated areas in the world with around 5,405 people to every square mile (14,000 per sq km).

Japanese homes are quite small. The home of a middle-class family of four only

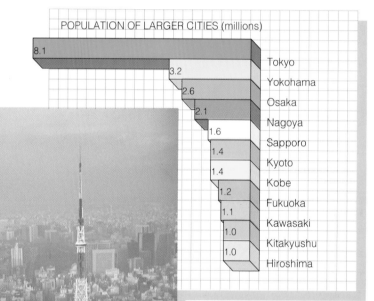

POPULATION OF LARGER CITIES (millions)

8.1	Tokyo
3.2	Yokohama
2.6	Osaka
2.1	Nagoya
1.6	Sapporo
1.4	Kyoto
1.4	Kobe
1.2	Fukuoka
1.1	Kawasaki
1.0	Kitakyushu
1.0	Hiroshima

◀ *Japan has 11 cities of over 1 million people. With the exception of Sapporo they are all in the south.*

▼ *Between 1870 and 1970 the population grew from 30 to 100 million. Now the increase is much less, only 0.3 percent a year.*

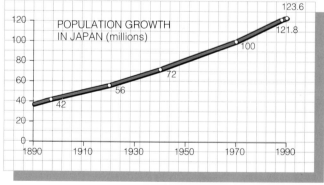

POPULATION GROWTH IN JAPAN (millions)

◀ *More than three-quarters of the population live in large cities like Tokyo and work in factories, shops, and offices. Like most modern cities, Tokyo has busy streets, tall office buildings, and large residential areas.*

has two or three rooms, plus a kitchen, and bathroom. The most common Japanese-style room is fitted with tatami mats made from tightly matted rice stalks. A large closet stores bedding. In the center of the room is a low table around which people sit. At night the table is moved aside and the bedding laid out on a futon on the floor. Most Japanese homes now have at least one Western-style room, usually the kitchen, which will often have a table and chairs like those in Western kitchens.

KEY FACTS

● Japan is the seventh most populated country in the world.
● About 99% of the population is Japanese, 0.6% Korean, and 0.2% Chinese and other nationalities.
● Tokyo, and the area around it, houses 30 million people, making it one of the largest metropolises in the world.
● There are almost 40 million homes in Japan.
● About 99% of Japanese homes have color TV sets.

▲Japanese homes are small. Rooms are designed so that different activities can take place at different times. They are simply decorated and furnished. Internal walls are thin and can slide back to create larger spaces.

Outside the cities some old villages and towns remain. Although most Japanese live in towns and cities, they still feel a strong attachment to the countryside.

An old Ainu man, a descendant of one of the original inhabitants of Japan.

THE AINU

When the first immigrants arrived from the Asian mainland, they found the islands of Japan already inhabited by a people known as the Ainu. Today there are only about 15,000 Ainu left, and they live mainly on the island of Hokkaido. They have their own language and cultural traditions but, like minority groups in many parts of the world, they feel neglected by the government.

DAILY LIFE

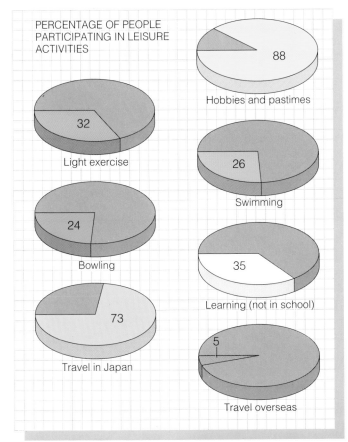

PERCENTAGE OF PEOPLE PARTICIPATING IN LEISURE ACTIVITIES

88 — Hobbies and pastimes

32 — Light exercise

26 — Swimming

24 — Bowling

35 — Learning (not in school)

73 — Travel in Japan

5 — Travel overseas

Western visitors to Japan often feel that the Japanese people are very different from themselves. The Japanese have a very ancient culture which, despite the influence of Western ideas over the past 40 years, remains very strong.

Compared to people in Western countries, the Japanese seem to enjoy the friendship of groups. They often work, relax, and worship with the same group. They often develop strong feelings of loyalty and duty to the members of their group. Most Japanese have a great respect for authority and are very honest. Tourists who have lost their luggage will almost always get it back — with their money intact!

EDUCATION

The Japanese education system is good but very competitive. Compulsory education starts at the age of six, but there is so much

▲ *The popularity of different leisure activities*

▶ *At school all children wear uniforms, study the same subjects, use the same textbooks, and take the same examinations. There is little time for them to develop individual personalities. Many parents now feel the system makes their children unhappy.*

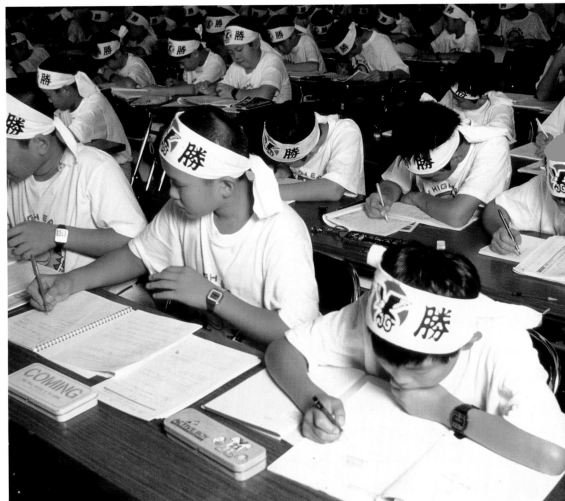

competition to get into the best schools that eight out of ten children go to kindergarten from the age of three. Elementary school lasts for six years and middle school for three years. These nine years of education are compulsory, but most children go to high school for another three years.

Homework is given from a very early age, and many children spend their summers at private schools so they will get into a university. One in three go on to a university.

RELIGION

The main religions in Japan are Shintoism and Buddhism. Most people combine beliefs and ceremonies from both in their daily lives. For example, most Japanese have a Shinto wedding but prefer a Buddhist funeral.

The Shinto religion is found only in Japan. Shinto means "way of the gods." The Japanese recognize millions of gods called KAMI who live in natural places, such as rivers, lakes, and trees. These sites are sacred, and each one has a shrine or temple. A gateway,

◀ *Buddhism developed in India and came to Japan in the 6th century A.D. Buddha means "the enlightened one." The Buddha was a living person who left his rich and powerful family to search for the meaning of life. After many years of poverty, he achieved his aim. Buddhists try to follow his teachings so they too can find the meaning of life. The Japanese feel that Shintoism prepares them for their daily life and that Buddhism prepares them for the afterlife.*

RELIGIOUS FESTIVALS AND HOLIDAYS

Festivals are associated with the rhythms of nature and religious beliefs.

January 1 NEW YEAR'S DAY
A national holiday. Most businesses close from January 1–3. This is the most important celebration of the year. Homes are decorated for a "long, strong, and prosperous year." There are special foods and gifts, and family visits.

January 15 ADULTS' DAY
There are ceremonies for everyone over the age of 20.

February 11 NATIONAL FOUNDATION DAY
A national holiday to celebrate when the first Japanese emperor, Jimmu Tenno, came to the throne in 660 B.C.

March 3 GIRLS' DAY
Not an official holiday but widely observed. Girls go to each others' homes to admire collections of dolls which are lovingly made by craftspeople and passed on from one generation to the next.

March 20 or 21 VERNAL EQUINOX DAY
A national holiday to celebrate the coming of spring. Visits are made to family graves.

April 29 GREENERY DAY
The beginning of "Golden Week" when most people take a whole week off work

May 3 CONSTITUTION DAY
A national holiday to commemorate the new constitution of 1947

May 5 CHILDREN'S DAY (formerly Boys' Day)
A national holiday. If there is a son in the family, a pole is erected in the garden with paper and carp-shaped cloth streamers attached. These are symbols of energy, determination, and ambition. There are also models of warriors.

August O-BON FESTIVAL
A day for visiting shrines and dancing. It is the night when the souls of the departed return to Earth.

September 15 RESPECT FOR THE AGED DAY

September 23 AUTUMNAL EQUINOX DAY
A national holiday to celebrate the approach of autumn and a day for visiting the family graves

October 10 SPORTS DAY OR PHYSICAL CULTURE DAY
Introduced to commemorate the holding of the Olympics in Tokyo in 1964

November 3 CULTURE DAY
A national holiday to encourage people to enjoy peace and culture. It was the birthday of Mutsuhito (Meiji) who was emperor from 1867–1912.

November 23 LABOR THANKSGIVING DAY
A national holiday often combined with harvest festivals. The emperor makes a ritual offering of SAKE to the gods.

December 23 THE EMPEROR'S BIRTHDAY

December 31 NEW YEAR'S EVE
Bells at important temples ring out 108 times at midnight to mark the end of the old year.

There are also many colorful regional and local festivals with processions and floats, singing, shouting, and dancing. For example, a festival is held in Kyoto during July to celebrate the founding of the city.

▲ *There are about 80,000 Shinto shrines, and every community has at least one. Prayers are often pinned up by visitors. Before exams, many students pin up prayers asking for good results.*

or TORRII, marks the entrance to the site. Visiting these sites is especially popular during annual festivals. Important historical figures, such as warriors, have also been regarded as gods. Until the end of World War II, Japan's emperor was worshipped as a god.

FAMILY LIFE

The average age of marriage is 28.3 years for men and 25.6 years for women. This is higher than in most industrial countries.

◀ *Baseball has become very popular, and Japan has the world's largest baseball leagues. The players are treated as stars, like top athletes all over the world.*

Marriages in Japan used to be arranged by matchmakers, but today this is rare.

The average work week is 41.5 hours, also higher than in other industrial countries. Workers are expected to go out with their colleagues after work. They will not get home until late, so a father sees little of his family except on Sunday. Even if a job allows two weeks of vacation a year, most workers do not take it all.

LEISURE ACTIVITIES

Many popular leisure activities, such as SUMO, JUDO, and KENDO, are part of Japanese culture. Others, such as golf and baseball, have been adopted from the West.

The most popular leisure activity is gardening. Even people living in apartments have a window box with plants. Almost every house has a small plot 6 feet by 6 feet (2 m by 2 m) which may contain just a single tree, one or two large rocks, and sand or gravel raked into patterns.

Japan also has a long tradition of different types of theater. These include BUNRAKU, KABUKI, and NOH.

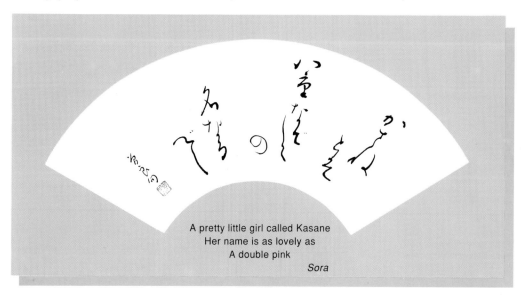

A pretty little girl called Kasane
Her name is as lovely as
A double pink
Sora

◀ *A type of poem that is unique to Japan is haiku. It usually consists of three short lines. This haiku was written by the poet Kawai Sora (1649–1710).*

KEY FACTS

- Ninety-four percent of the children stay in school until the age of 18.
- Only 1 in 5 university students are women.
- Two workers in five are women, but their average pay is half that of men.
- Japan produced the world's first novel around A.D. 1000.
- The percentage of members of religions in Japan is:

Shinto	39.5
Buddhism	38.3
Christian	3.8
Others	18.4

▲ Two girls wear the traditional KIMONO during a festival which celebrates reaching seven years of age. The OBI holds the gowns in place.

◄ Sumo wrestling is an ancient sport and is celebrated here at a festival. A wrestler or RIKISHI weighs over 286 pounds (130 kg).

RULES AND LAWS

As early as 200 B.C., people were living in villages and farming in the area we now know as Japan. Japan has been ruled by emperors who, until 1946, were regarded as gods descended from Amaterasu, the Sun goddess. However, for much of the time the emperors had little power. The country was controlled by the SHOGUN, the head of one of three powerful families. The shoguns controlled the warriors known as SAMURAI and ruled the country as they liked.

In 1867 the emperor Mutsuhito regained power from the shoguns. He opened Japan to Western ideas, which the shoguns had excluded for over 200 years.

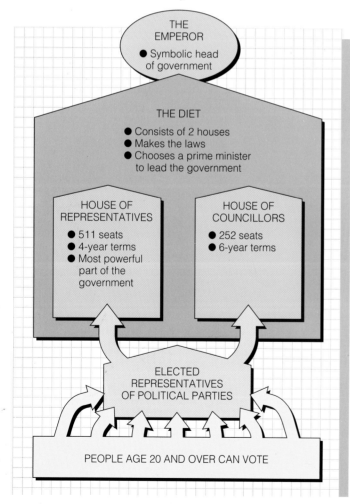

THE EMPEROR
● Symbolic head of government

THE DIET
● Consists of 2 houses
● Makes the laws
● Chooses a prime minister to lead the government

HOUSE OF REPRESENTATIVES
● 511 seats
● 4-year terms
● Most powerful part of the government

HOUSE OF COUNCILLORS
● 252 seats
● 6-year terms

ELECTED REPRESENTATIVES OF POLITICAL PARTIES

PEOPLE AGE 20 AND OVER CAN VOTE

▲ *Anyone over age 20 can vote for politicians to represent them in the national government.*

▼ *Under the constitution introduced after World War II, Japan will not settle international conflicts by war.*

CHAPTER II. RENUNCIATION OF WAR

ARTICLE 9. Aspiring sincerely to an international peace based on justice and order, the Japanese people forever renounce war as a sovereign right of the nation and the threat or use of force as means of settling international disputes.

In order to accomplish the aim of the preceding paragraph, land, sea, and air forces, as well as other war potential, will never be maintained. The right of belligerency of the state will not be recognized.

Japan became stronger and occupied several countries in Asia, including Korea and parts of Russia and China. It fought against the Allies in World War II and finally surrendered when atomic bombs were dropped on Hiroshima and Nagasaki in 1945.

The United States occupied Japan from 1945 to 1952. A new constitution was drawn up. Hirohito (emperor from 1926 to 1989) remained the ruler, but he became a constitutional monarch, like the king or queen of Great Britain. When he died in 1989, his son Akihito became emperor.

The country is divided into 47 prefectures. Each has a governor and an assembly of elected people providing local government.

KEY FACTS

● Nippon (or Nihon) is the Japanese word for Japan. It means "source of the sun."
● In 1945 General Douglas MacArthur ordered Emperor Hirohito to state publicly that he was not a god.
● There are few murders in Japan, only 1.4 a year for every 100,000 people. In the United States there are 8.7.

▼*Japanese people are very law abiding, and there is little robbery or violence. Community spirit is strong, and the police are part of the community.*

FOOD AND FARMING

arms are very small, usually only 2 to 5 acres (1 or 2 ha). A farmer may have three or four fields in different places around the village.

Rice is the most widely grown crop. The chief growing area used to be the warm island of Kyushu in the south where two crops a year can be grown. New varieties of rice can now be grown in the cooler climate of northern Honshu, and this area has become more important than Kyushu. Other crops include tomatoes, eggplants, carrots, sweet potatoes, onions, watermelons, and strawberries.

The slopes above the PADDY FIELDS are terraced to make small level fields. Here farmers plant grains, such as wheat and barley, or trees and bushes. Apples and pears are grown in the cooler north, while tea, mandarins, tangerines, peaches, and nectarines are grown in the south.

Traditionally farmers have not kept animals for food but eating habits are changing. Today large numbers of poultry are kept for their meat and eggs. In the south of Japan a farmer might keep a few beef cattle. The meat from these animals is very expensive because there is so little grazing, and the cattle are hand-reared. The meat is used in dishes such as SUKIYAKI.

◀ *Fish is eaten at most meals. Japan's fishing fleet is the world's largest. It catches 13 million tons a year, about one-eighth of all fish caught in the world.*

KEY FACTS

● In Japan there is only 0.1 acre (0.04 ha) of farmland for each person.
● Most cities now have Western-style eating places. Family meals are more traditional.
● Raw fish dishes, such as SUSHI and SASHIMI, are very

popular. So is the poisonous FUGU.

● Mulberry trees cover 222,390 acres (90,000 ha) of land, mainly in central Honshu. The leaves feed silkworms, which produce 44,090 tons of silk a year.

▲Rice is the main food and is eaten at almost every meal. It is grown on about half of all farmland. Farms and fields are small, so large modern machinery cannot be used.

▼The evening family meal is generally a traditional Japanese one eaten with chopsticks. Western-style diets are increasingly common.

Hokkaido is becoming an important agricultural area. Its cool, moist climate provides excellent pasture for dairy cattle and the crops grown are suitable for Western-style diets.

The Japanese eat three times as much fish as meat. Fishing has always been important. The fishing fleets go to the Pacific, Indian, and Atlantic oceans. Japanese farmers often breed fish in ponds and tanks on their farms. Now fish farms have also been set up just off the shore. Edible seaweed is also very popular.

The Japanese still hunt whales for "scientific purposes." Whale meat is another popular delicacy, but it can cost $100 per pound.

▲ *Attractive presentation of food is important in Japanese cuisine. Lunch boxes are no exception!*

▶ *Japan produces 70 percent of its food. Farms are tiny, so most farmers have another job.*

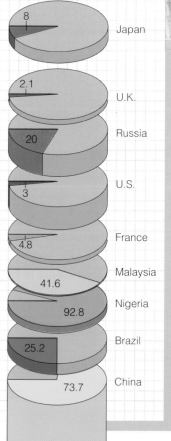

PERCENTAGE OF WORK FORCE IN AGRICULTURE
(depth = no. in work force)

8	Japan
2.1	U.K.
20	Russia
3	U.S.
4.8	France
41.6	Malaysia
92.8	Nigeria
25.2	Brazil
73.7	China

TRADE AND INDUSTRY

In just over 100 years Japan has changed from a poor farming country to a rich industrial one. Before 1868, there were only a few small factories making products like silk, paper, and pottery. Emperor Mutsuhito, now usually known as Meiji, introduced Western ideas and technology. He modernized agriculture, opened coal and copper mines, improved roads, and built railroads. From 1880 to the 1930s, Japan produced its own textiles, steel, machinery, and vehicles, but few were exported.

The most spectacular industrial growth has taken place since 1950. The main industries of Europe and America now face stiff competition from the Japanese. The first industry to suffer from Japanese competition was shipbuilding, then motorcycles, cars, and other vehicles, cameras, electrical goods, electronic equipment, and musical instruments. In fact,

▲ *This oil refinery in Tokyo Bay is built on land reclaimed from the sea. Japan imports crude oil and turns it into products such as gasoline, diesel fuel, and oil.*

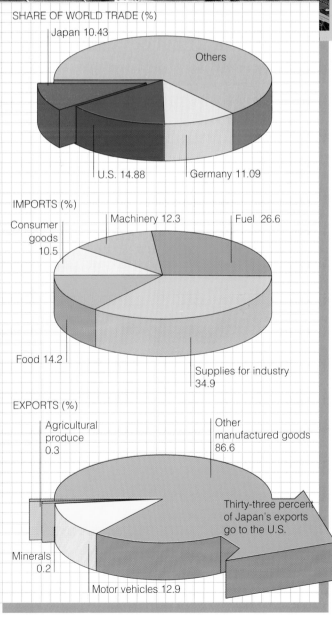

SHARE OF WORLD TRADE (%)
Japan 10.43
Others
U.S. 14.88   Germany 11.09

IMPORTS (%)
Consumer goods 10.5
Machinery 12.3
Fuel 26.6
Food 14.2
Supplies for industry 34.9

EXPORTS (%)
Agricultural produce 0.3
Other manufactured goods 86.6
Thirty-three percent of Japan's exports go to the U.S.
Minerals 0.2
Motor vehicles 12.9

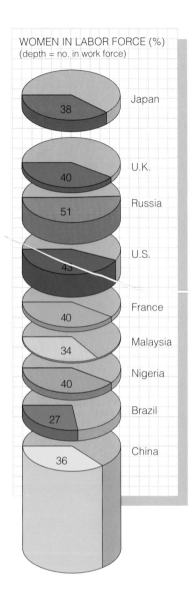

WOMEN IN LABOR FORCE (%)
(depth = no. in work force)

- Japan — 38
- U.K. — 40
- Russia — 51
- U.S. — 45
- France — 40
- Malaysia — 34
- Nigeria — 40
- Brazil — 27
- China — 36

▶ *Japan is the world's biggest producer of electrical and electronic goods.*

Japan now makes most types of industrial goods. Japanese companies are very successful because they invest large sums of money developing new products, have good management and loyal employees, produce high quality goods, have millions of customers in Japan, and have been encouraged to sell their products abroad.

THE IRON AND STEEL INDUSTRY

The steel industry is the foundation of modern Japan. Steel is used in buildings, ships, vehicles, and most consumer goods. Production has increased from 5.5 million tons a year in 1950 to around 117 million tons a year today.

Japan imports 99 percent of its iron ore. Australia provides about 40 percent, Brazil

▶*Japanese companies are setting up factories in the countries where they sell many of their goods. This car factory in Great Britain has been so successful it is being expanded.*

25 percent, and India 20 percent. The other raw material needed is coal, and Japan has to import about 96 percent of this. About 66 million tons are imported a year, 26 million from Australia, 18 million from Canada, and 11 million from the U.S. Around 33 million tons of steel are exported, mainly to China, Taiwan, South Korea, and the U.S.

The main steel-making plants have been built along the southern coast of Honshu, between Tokyo and Hiroshima. Some, like the one in Oita on Kyushu, are built on land reclaimed from the sea.

THE SHIPBUILDING INDUSTRY

Half the ships sailing today were built in Japan. In the 1960s and 1970s, huge shipyards made the ships Japan needed to take raw materials and manufactured goods to and from the rest of the world. These yards built the first oil supertankers.

The shipyards were built close to the steel works because steel is used to make ships. The industry has declined since its peak in the mid-1970s, but it still builds about 40 percent of the world's ships.

AUTOMOBILE INDUSTRY

The first Japanese-made cars arrived in the U.S. and Europe during the 1960s. At first, car manufacturers did not consider them serious competitors. Today, however, Japan has the largest motor industry of any country, producing about 9.7 million cars and 7.6 million trucks and buses a year. About half of these are sold abroad, mainly to North America and Europe. Giant ships capable of holding 6,000 cars transport Japanese cars to overseas markets.

The automobile industry has been very successful. It employs around 5 million people in Japan alone. Mitsubishi, one of the biggest manufacturers, now builds vehicles in more than 30 countries and sells them in about 160.

ELECTRICAL GOODS

Japan decided to switch from heavy industries, like iron- and steel-making and

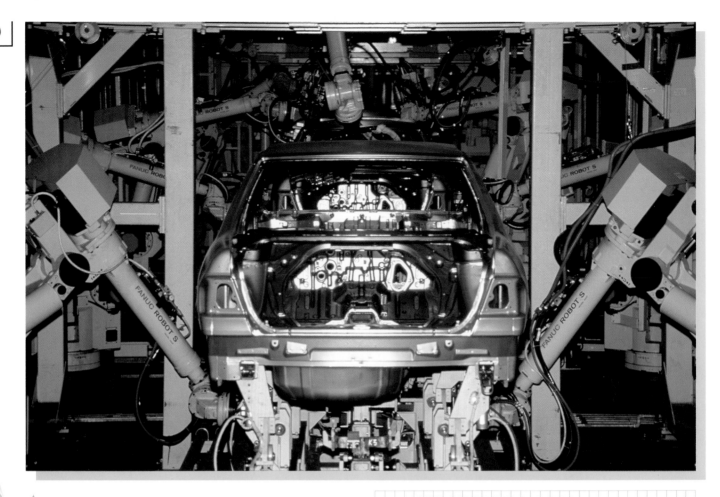

▲*Robots do much of the building and painting in this car factory. They cost less than people and can work in unhealthy environments.*

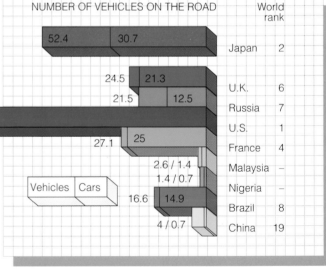

NUMBER OF VEHICLES ON THE ROAD		World rank
52.4	30.7	Japan — 2
24.5	21.3	U.K. — 6
21.5	12.5	Russia — 7
183.5	140.6	U.S. — 1
27.1	25	France — 4
2.6 / 1.4		Malaysia — —
1.4 / 0.7		Nigeria — —
16.6	14.9	Brazil — 8
4 / 0.7		China — 19

Vehicles | Cars

KEY FACTS

● On an assembly line, one car is completed every 43 seconds.
● There are factories in Japan where robots are making more robots.
● An employee of a big company expects to work for that company for life.
● Seven of the world's 10 largest banks are all Japanese.

shipbuilding, because they depended on imported raw materials and energy supplies. Instead, they developed industries like the electrical industry, which needs a well-educated work force but few raw materials.

The output of electrical goods is immense. In 1990 Japan produced 352 million watches, 68 million calculators, 29 million stereo

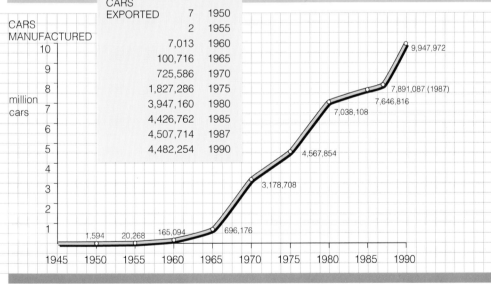

NUMBER OF CARS EXPORTED	Year
7	1950
2	1955
7,013	1960
100,716	1965
725,586	1970
1,827,286	1975
3,947,160	1980
4,426,762	1985
4,507,714	1987
4,482,254	1990

CARS MANUFACTURED

million cars

9,947,972
7,891,087 (1987)
7,646,816
7,038,108
4,567,854
3,178,708
696,176
1,594   20,268   165,094

▲ *Japanese companies spend large sums of money developing new products. This car has a computer to help the driver avoid traffic jams. In the future all cars may have one, thereby increasing the company's revenue.*

systems, 28 million video recorders, 13 million color TVs, 6 million microwave ovens, 4 million FAX machines, 2.5 million computers, and 56,000 industrial robots.

These figures do not include all the electrical products put together in Japanese factories in neighboring countries, such as Taiwan, Malaysia, South Korea, and Hong Kong, where wages and other costs are lower. However, the research into improving products and making new ones is still carried out in Japan. Japanese companies also find it profitable to establish factories in countries where they sell the most goods, such as the U.S. or the U.K.

Japanese companies are always searching for new products to make and export. Having started with electric organs and keyboards, Japan now produces high quality musical instruments, including pianos, harps, violins, and guitars. Japan is one of the biggest manufacturers of electrical goods in the world and a producer of world-class competition motorcycles.

WORKING FOR A JAPANESE COMPANY

Industry in Japan is dominated by a few large companies, such as Toyota or Mitsubishi. When people go to work for them, they become part of a "family" and expect to be cared for by the company for life. Companies often have whole suburbs or small cities for their employees to live in where housing is often more affordable. Companies may provide scholarships for the children of employees, health care, annual parties, and even annual vacations. In return, the companies expect loyalty and hard work.

In the factories there are no big divisions between the management and the factory workers. The views of people on all levels in the company are valued. There are no strikes.

▲The stock exchange in Tokyo is where companies and individuals can buy and sell shares in Japan's companies. Banking, insurance, and other financial services employ more than two million people. The currency used in Japan is the yen.

東京証券取引所

TOKYO STOCK EXCHANGE

TRANSPORTATION

Although made up of islands, Japan has an extremely efficient transportation system. Roads and railroads are the main carriers. Ferry and air services link the smaller islands.

Like large cities in all developed countries, the roads are clogged with vehicles, especially at rush hours. Most people use the local trains or subways in major cities, like Tokyo. They are among the most efficient and overcrowded in the world.

An excellent railroad network links the major cities. Besides the government-owned Japan Railways, there are also private railroad companies. Japan pioneered high-speed trains in the 1960s, and today there are three high-speed lines, which all start from Tokyo. The first line was built to the west. It links Tokyo with other industrial centers, such as Nagoya and Osaka, and terminates in Fukuoka on Kyushu. Another

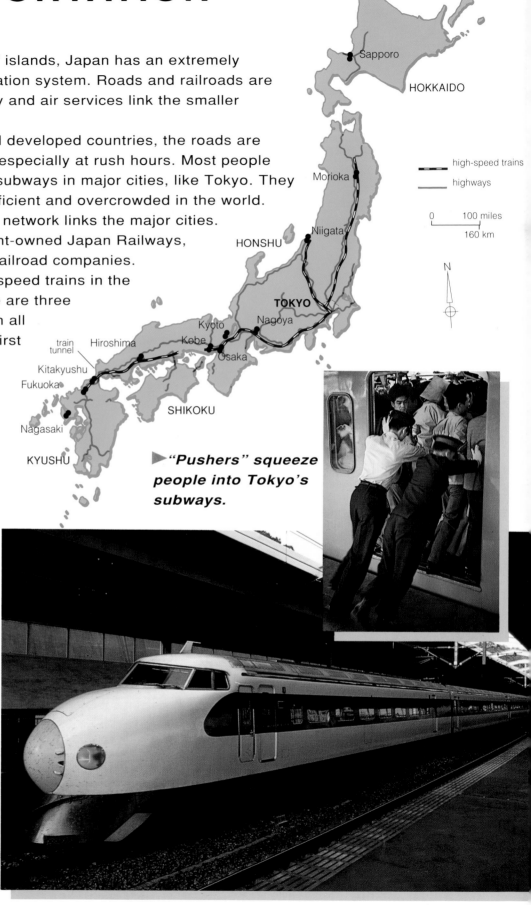

▶ *"Pushers" squeeze people into Tokyo's subways.*

▶ *Japan's high-speed "bullet train" can travel at 140 mph (240 kph). It travels between Tokyo and Osaka in 3 hours.*

RATIO OF PEOPLE PER CAR	
3.3	Japan
2.9	U.K.
22.6	Russia
1.7	U.S.
2.4	France
12.1	Malaysia
119	Nigeria
10.5	Brazil
1.577	China

high-speed trains

highways

0   100 miles
      160 km

N

Sapporo

HOKKAIDO

Morioka

Niigata

HONSHU

TOKYO

Nagoya

Kyoto
Kobe
Osaka

train tunnel   Hiroshima

Kitakyushu
Fukuoka

SHIKOKU

Nagasaki

KYUSHU

line runs north across the country to Niigata and a third northeast to Morioka in the north of Honshu.

The road system is being improved constantly to cope with the 30.7 million cars and 21.4 million trucks that use it. Highways now link all the major cities. Roads carry 93 percent of all freight.

Tunnels and bridges join the four major islands. The Seikan Tunnel between Honshu and Hokkaido is 27 miles (43 km) long and is the longest underwater train tunnel until the Channel Tunnel between France and the U.K. opens. The longest suspension bridge in the world is being built in Japan. The Akashi-Kaikyo Road Bridge is due for completion in 1998. Its overall span will measure 6,529 feet (1,990 m) across and it will link the islands of Honshu and Shikoku.

▲ *Huge bridges have been built to speed up travel between Japan's islands. The Seto-Ohashi Bridge links several of the smaller islands.*

KEY FACTS

● The Japanese drive on the left side of the road.
● There are 17,049 miles (27,454 km) of railroad and over 650,000 miles (1.1 million km) of roads.
● The railroads carry almost 21 million intercity passengers a year and 91 million tons of freight.
● Japan is the only country in the world which uses jumbo jets for internal passenger flights due to the high number of people wishing to travel.

Japan has become a very wealthy country because its industries have been extremely successful. Until recently, few people, in Japan or any other industrialized country, realized it was important to protect the environment. People and the environment suffered as a result. Now Japan has some of the strictest antipollution laws in the world.

In and around the cities the air is badly polluted by the fumes from factories and vehicles. Doctors now recognize diseases caused by pollution, such as Yokkaichi asthma suffered by people living near the Yokkaichi chemical works in Kawasaki.

Many rivers in the industrial areas are so badly polluted by factories that they can no longer be used to supply drinking water. In

▲ *Away from the cities much of the country is wild and beautiful. National parks, like this one at Takao near Kyoto, have been set up in all parts of Japan to protect the countryside from development.*

▼ *Sulfur dioxide and nitrogen oxides are the main causes of acid rain.*

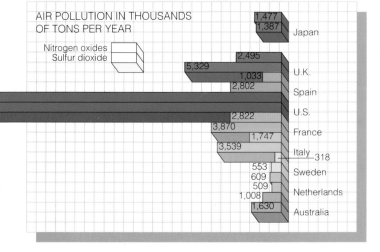

AIR POLLUTION IN THOUSANDS OF TONS PER YEAR

Nitrogen oxides
Sulfur dioxide

Country	Nitrogen oxides	Sulfur dioxide
Japan	1,477	1,387
U.K.	2,495	5,329
Spain	1,033	2,802
U.S.	22,371	26,358
France	2,822	3,870
Italy	1,747	3,539 / 318
Sweden	553	609
Netherlands	509	1,008
Australia	1,630	

1971 people living near the Toruku Mine on Kyushu became very ill because their water had been poisoned with arsenic used in the mine. People are still suffering and dying from its effects.

The polluted water from industry and the cities ends up in the sea. Seafood, such as oysters and fish, caught in these waters can be dangerous to eat. One of the worst pollution disasters ever was in Minamata City on Kyushu. Mercury from a chemical works was allowed to run into the sea where it was consumed by sea creatures. When these were eaten, the poison was also eaten by people. Affected people could not see, hear, or speak properly and lost their sense of touch. Over 750 have died since 1953 when the disease, now known as Minamata disease, was first recognized.

KEY FACTS

● Japan has 55 million tons of waste to dispose of a year.
● The Kawasaki milk carton recycling group collects old milk cartons to turn into toilet paper.
● In major cities 30% of the drinking water wells are contaminated with chemicals and unfit for drinking.

▲ *Japan is one of the few countries that still hunts whales. In 1991 the whaling fleet set out to catch 330 minke whales in the Antarctic. Commercial whaling is banned, but the whales are killed, so it is said, to allow scientists to learn more about them.*

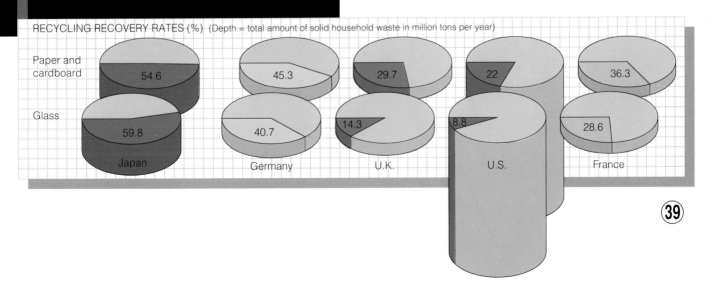

RECYCLING RECOVERY RATES (%) (Depth = total amount of solid household waste in million tons per year)

	Japan	Germany	U.K.	U.S.	France
Paper and cardboard	54.6	45.3	29.7	22	36.3
Glass	59.8	40.7	14.3	8.8	28.6

Half of Japan's population lives along the Kanto Plain. The towns are spread over huge areas, and getting from one place to another creates terrible congestion and air pollution. This is a highway out of Tokyo at the height of the evening rush hour, though from the size of the traffic jam, "rush" is not the right word!

Japan has been criticized by international environmental groups, like Greenpeace and the World Wide Fund for Nature, for failing to protect the environment. People were recently shocked by pictures from the island of Fukue of fishermen clubbing more than 500 dolphins to death, supposedly to protect their fish.

However, pressure for environmental protection is growing rapidly. People living on the Shiraho coral reef off the island of Ishigaki fought for 11 years to prevent a new airport from being built on the reef and destroying its unique wildlife. The airport will still be built but on another coral reef where it will do less harm.

As stricter laws go into effect, the amount of air pollution is decreasing. Factories have to clean their smoke before it goes into the air. As a result, the air in some cities contains only one-sixth of the sulfur dioxide it did in the 1960s. All new cars are fitted with catalytic converters, which reduce pollution from car exhausts. Japan is also trying to save resources by recycling paper and glass.

THE FUTURE

Japan has come a long way since the end of World War II. Then, to help the country recover, Japanese industries were protected from imported foreign goods. This is still the case. No one then imagined that before the end of the century, Japan would be the world's leading industrial nation. In fact, when Japanese goods started to arrive in Western countries in the 1960s, they were described as cheap and inferior. People never dreamed that within 30 years other countries would be trying to copy Japan's economic example. Today, Japan makes two-thirds of all computer chips and electronic consumer goods. Its economic power dominates the world. It owns more businesses and property in overseas countries than any other country, including the United States.

Japan has the world's leading stock exchange and the largest trade surplus ever known. A country has a trade surplus when it earns more money from what it sells overseas than what it spends on buying things from overseas. Each year Japan exports goods worth $275 billion and imports goods worth $210 billion, giving it a very large trade surplus indeed. Some of the main importing countries, such as the United States and Great Britain, complain that the Japanese are unfair and make it difficult for countries trying to sell goods in Japan, while Japanese goods can be sold in other countries without difficulty. As a result, many countries now limit the number of Japanese goods they import.

Another complaint is that Japanese goods are cheaper than similar ones made in the West. These goods are not made in Japan but in neighboring countries where wages are lower than in Japan or the West. Japanese companies are also criticized for showing little respect for the peoples or environments of the countries from which they import resources like coal and timber.

◄ *Japan uses advanced forms of computer graphics to illustrate new ideas in design and technology. Here is a representation of a new building that will be constructed using robots.*

◀ *These teenagers are among many who are trying to break away from the strict traditions of their parents. The music and clothing styles of the West have a strong influence on Japanese youth today.*

Another criticism is that Japan is a wealthy country but takes little part in international events, such as the Persian Gulf War, or peace-keeping in other countries. However, Japan does give more aid to developing countries than any other country. The Japanese have been hurt by these criticisms, and there are signs that they are changing their policies.

Apart from their relationship with other countries, the Japanese face a serious problem at home: overcrowding and lack of space. Japanese architects and engineers have proposed some fantastic solutions. One is to build cities stretching high into the sky.

Japan is not the only country with the problem of overcrowding. In 1994 the country will host a world conference and exhibition that will look at living in cities in the 21st century. Twenty million visitors are expected to attend.

The economic and industrial success of Japan since the destruction caused by World War II has been phenomenal. Although there are hints that some young people in Japan are beginning to question their highly organized, highly competitive way of life, it may be a very long time before Japan loses its economic supremacy.

KEY FACTS

● The population balance will change by the year 2000. In 1980, 9% of the population was age 65 or over. In 2000 this figure will be 15.6%.

● It is expected that by the year 2000, the number of old people receiving pensions will be about four times more than in 1980.

● Japan will continue in the 1990s with research and development "offshore" (not within Japan).

▲*Young designers are encouraged to create fantastic vehicles at the Toyota Idea Expo. The "Neo Cosmic Voyager"* *shown here can hug the ground like a sports car or raise itself up to move over obstacles.*

FURTHER INFORMATION

JAPAN AIRLINES
655 Fifth Avenue, New York, NY 10022
JAPAN NATIONAL TOURIST OFFICE
360 Post Street, San Francisco, CA 94108
JAPAN NATIONAL TOURIST
ORGANIZATION
Rockefeller Plaza, 650 Fifth Avenue,
New York, NY 10111
JAPANESE EMBASSY
2520 Massachusetts Avenue, N.W.,
Washington, DC 20008

BOOKS ABOUT JAPAN
Allen, Carol. *Japan.* Good Apple, 1992
Dudley, William, ed. *Japan: Opposing Viewpoints.* Greenhaven, 1989
Greene, Carol. *Japan.* Childrens, 1983

James, Richard. *Japan: The Land and Its People.* Silver Burdett, 1987
Kalman, Bobbie. *Japan: The Land.* Crabtree, 1989
Lerner Publications, Department of Geography Staff. *Japan in Pictures.* Lerner, 1989
Meeks, Christopher. *Japan.* Rourke Corp, 1990
Meyer, Carolyn. *A Voice from Japan: An Outsider Looks In.* Harcourt Brace Jovanovich, 1992
Pilbeam, Mavis. *Japan.* Trafalgar, 1992
Stefoff, Rebecca. *Japan.* Chelsea, 1988
Takeshita, Jiro. *Food in Japan.* Rourke Corp., 1989
Uchida, Yoshiko. *Samurai of Gold Hill.* Creative Arts Bk., 1985

GLOSSARY

BUNRAKU
Stage plays acted by puppets accompanied by a storyteller and musician

FUGU
A poisonous blowfish

JUDO
A form of wrestling. Two contestants stand on a mat 29 feet (9 m) square. They score points by performing various locks, holds, or throws against their opponent.

KABUKI
Plays written from the 17th century onward about ancient legends of love and war. All the women's roles are played by men.

KAMI
The Shinto spirits which live in sacred places on Earth, such as rivers and lakes

KENDO
Coming from samurai sword fighting, contestants use bamboo staffs or wooden swords to try to strike precise target areas on each others' bodies.

KIMONO
The traditional dress of Japanese men and women dating from the 7th century. The ankle-length dress is normally silk and has long broad sleeves. It wraps over in front and is tied with an obi. Now kimonos are mainly worn by women on special occasions.

NOH
Plays about the old-fashioned life of Japanese aristocrats. The actors wear elaborate masks.

OBI
The wide waist sash used to tie a kimono

PADDY FIELDS
Fields in which rice is grown. Rice is a marsh plant. Paddy fields are surrounded by low banks and flooded.

RIKISHI
A sumo wrestler. He can weigh over 286 pounds (130 kg) but is very agile.

SAKE
An alcoholic drink made from rice. It is often drunk warm.

SAMURAI
The soldiers who formed a ruling class in Japan until the 19th century

SASHIMI
A meal of pieces of raw fish

SHOGUN
Military rulers who controlled the emperor and ruled Japan for nearly 700 years

SUKIYAKI
A meal made with thin strips of beef, vegetables, and seasoning. It is usually cooked at the table and eaten immediately.

SUMO
A form of wrestling. Two *rikishi* in a circular ring each try to make his opponent step outside the ring or touch the ground with part of his body other than the feet.

SUSHI
A special meal of cold rice and raw fish

TORRII
The elaborate gateways close to many Shinto shrines.

YEN
The currency used in Japan. One yen is divided into 100 sen — a unit seldom used today.

INDEX

© Simon & Schuster Young Books 1992

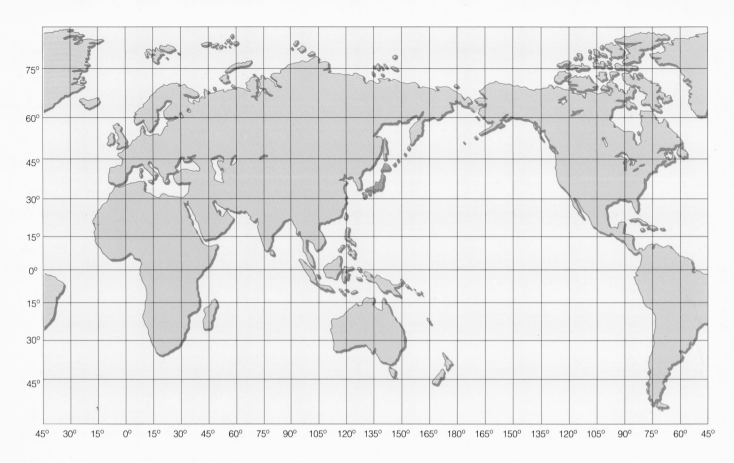

45° 30° 15° 0° 15° 30° 45° 60° 75° 90° 105° 120° 135° 150° 165° 180° 165° 150° 135° 120° 105° 90° 75° 60° 45°

129°

EAST

CHINA

SEA

RYUKYU ISLANDS

28°

OKINAWA

N

W   E

S